JAZZ GUITAR MASTERY

Transcribed by Chris Ullrich
Cover photo © Kevin Merrill

Online Video

To Access the Online Video Go to:

www.melbay.com/20770V – YouTube
or
dv.melbay.com/20770 - Download Video

1 2 3 4 5 6 7 8 9 0

TABLE OF CONTENTS

Foreword • 3

John Stowell - Jazz Mastery Volume I • 4

Pentatonics and Arpeggios • 5

Substitution Using Triads • 7

Picking • 11

Pick and Fingers Technique • 11

John Stowell - Jazz Mastery Volume II • 14

C7 + C$\sharp$ Melodic Minor • 19

One Whole Tone Below C7 • 21

C7 - F Melodic Minor a 4th Above > $\flat$6 added • 25

C7 - G Melodic Minor a 5th Above > 9 $\sharp$11 added • 27

John Stowell - Jazz Mastery Volume III • 30

Using Major Triads to Extend Dominant 7th Chord • 33

Dominant 7th Chords • 35

Major 7th Chords • 37

John Stowell • 38

FOREWORD

Hopefully my take on jazz as it applies to the guitar will offer some fresh perspective and inspiration. We're all students: practice new material in a shared environment with other like-minded players, learning and solving problems together. Some thanks: to my first teachers, guitarist Linc Chamberland and pianist John Mehegan, who got me started in jazz and were both very supportive; to Mike Gillette and Jennifer Hutchings at New Media for their original filming; to Chris Ullrich for beautifully accomplishing his long and difficult task of transcribing my material; to everybody at Mel Bay, Corey Christiansen for getting the ball rolling, to Bill Bay, Doug Witherspoon, Jon Hansen, Sheri Schleusner, Julie Price and John Purse for their assistance. Comments or questions are welcome.

John Stowell
Portland, Oregon, February, 2005
www.johnstowell.com

Chapter 1

"John Stowell—Jazz Mastery Volume I"

—*Transcribed by Chris Ullrich*—

1. Be able to take any sound and outline it in five places on the neck.

2. Practice random combinations of these five areas.

EXAMPLE 1: 2ND POSITION C MAJOR SCALE

EXAMPLE 2: 5TH POSITION C MAJOR SCALE

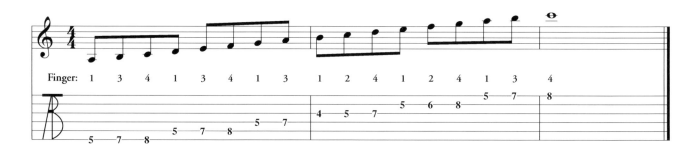

EXAMPLE 3: COMBINING 2ND + 5TH POSITION C MAJOR SCALE USING THE D STRING FOR TRANSITION—ASCENDING

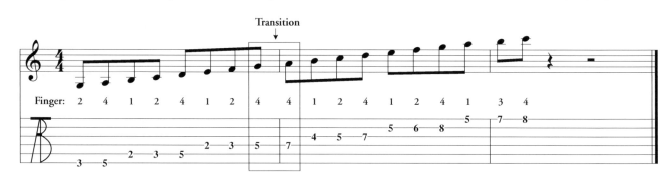

EXAMPLE 4: COMBINING 2ND + 5TH POSITION C MAJOR SCALE USING THE D STRING FOR TRANSITION—ASCENDING AND DESCENDING

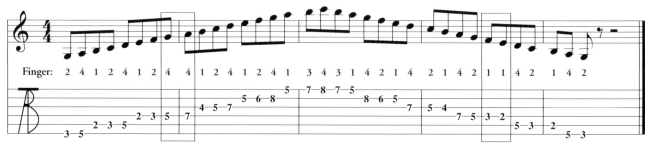

EXAMPLE 5: 2ND + 5TH POSITION C MAJOR SCALE USING THE G STRING FOR TRANSITION

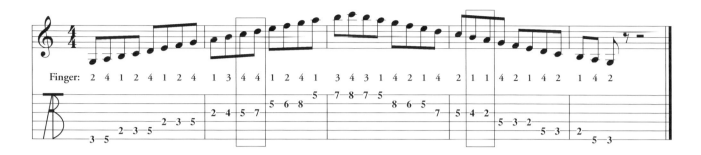

EXAMPLE 6: COMBINING THREE POSITIONS; 2ND, 5TH AND 7TH POSITION C MAJOR SCALE USING THE D AND G STRINGS FOR TRANSITIONS

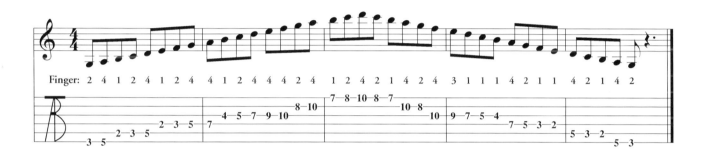

PENTATONICS AND ARPEGGIOS

DVD Chapter 2

1. Pentatonic = R 2 3 5 6 — C D E G A

2. Arpeggio = R 3 5 7 — C E G B

EXAMPLE 7: C MAJOR ARPEGGIO—2ND POSITION

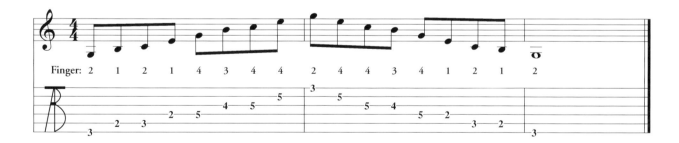

EXAMPLE 8: C MAJOR ARPEGGIO—2ND POSITION

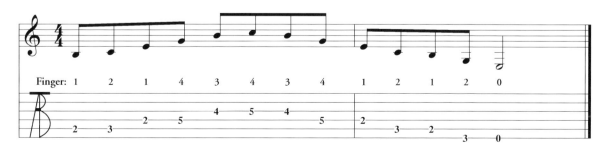

EXAMPLE 9: C MAJOR PENTATONIC

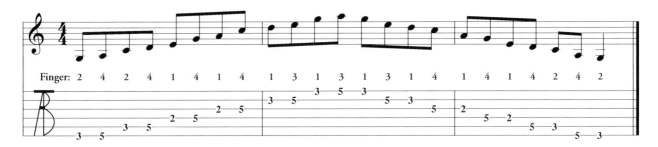

Finger: 2 4 2 4 1 4 1 4 1 3 1 3 1 3 1 4 1 4 1 4 2 4 2 2

EXAMPLE 10: COMBINING C MAJOR SCALE, ARPEGGIO AND PENTATONIC SCALE

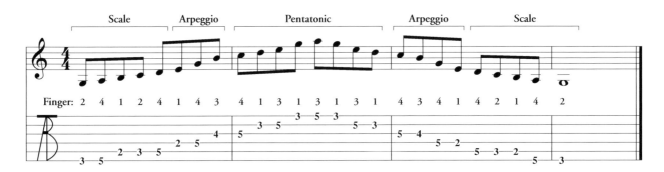

Scale   Arpeggio   Pentatonic   Arpeggio   Scale

Finger: 2 4 1 2 4 1 4 3 4 1 3 1 3 1 3 1 4 3 4 1 4 2 1 4 2

EXAMPLE 11:

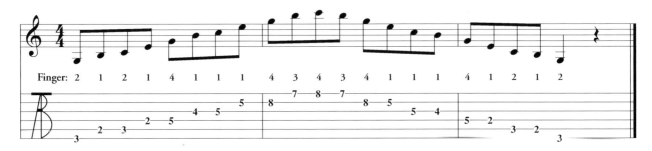

Finger: 2 1 2 1 4 1 1 1 4 3 4 3 4 1 1 1 4 1 2 1 2

EXAMPLE 12:

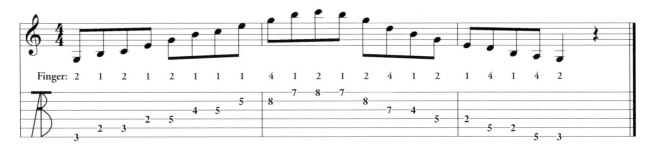

Finger: 2 1 2 1 2 1 1 1 4 1 2 1 2 4 1 2 1 4 1 4 2

EXAMPLE 13: CONNECTING PENTATONICS

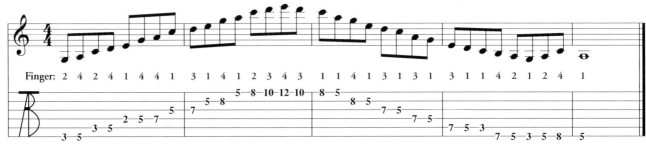

Finger: 2 4 2 4 1 4 4 1 3 1 4 1 2 3 4 3 1 1 4 1 3 1 3 1 3 1 1 4 2 1 2 4 1

6

Example 14:

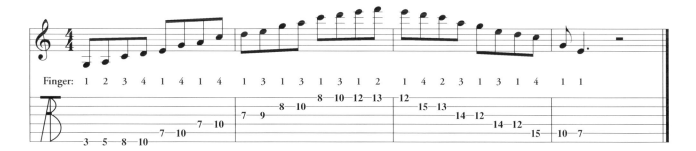

 Chapter 3

Substitution Using Triads

1. There are four notes outside of the Cmaj7 chord which you can add to Cmaj7 to achieve harmonic variety. The 6th which is an A, the 9th which is a D, and two notes outside of the C major scale, the ♯5 which is G♯ and the ♭5 which is G♭.

2. Using these four notes in conjunction with the C major scale allows us to use five major triads as substitutions for Cmaj7.

Example 15:

Cmaj7 — Play a **C** major triad which gives you the **R, 3, 5**

Play a **D** major triad which gives you the **9, ♭5,(♯11), 6**

Play an **E** major triad which gives you the **3, ♯5, 7**

Play an **F** major triad which gives you the **4, 6, R**

Play a **G** major triad which gives you the **5, 7, 9**

—In other words, on any major chord you can play a triad starting from the: Tonic

⇧ a major 2nd

⇧ a major 3rd

⇧ a perfect 4th

⇧ a perfect 5th

Example 16:

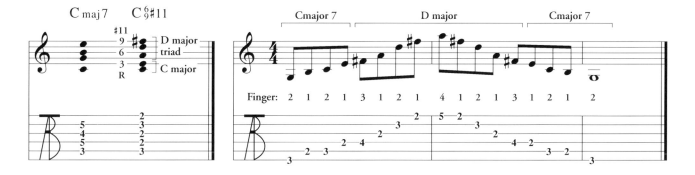

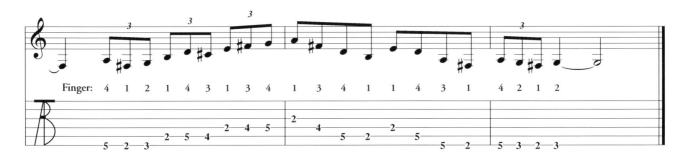

Example 18:

Example 19: E Major Triad as Cmajor7

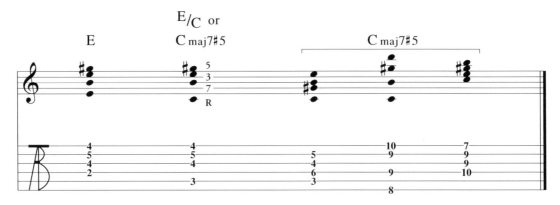

Example 20: Using the E Major Triad to Create Lines Over Cmajor 7

EXAMPLE 21:

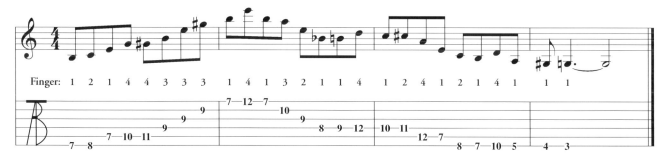

EXAMPLE 22a: USING THE F MAJOR TRIAD AS CMAJOR7

EXAMPLE 22b: HARMONIC MOVEMENT OUTLINED

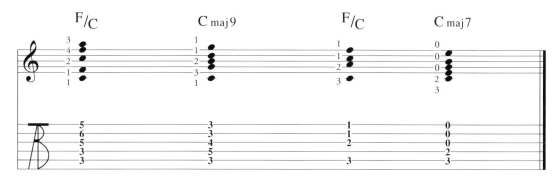

EXAMPLE 23:

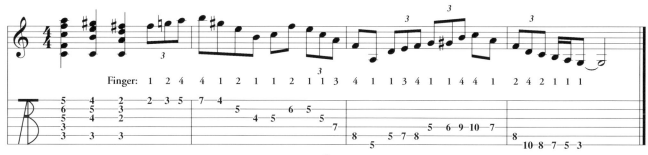

Example 24: Using the G Major Triad as Cmajor7

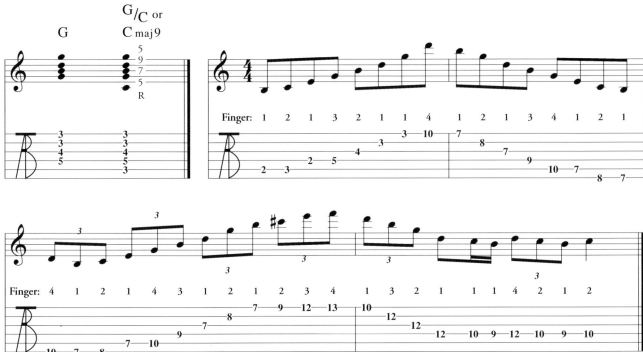

Example 25:

Chapter 4

PICKING

EXAMPLE 26:

⊓ = Downstroke V = Upstroke

PICK AND FINGERS TECHNIQUE

1. The right-hand fingers are designated by the of their Spanish names:

English Name	Spanish Name	Symbol
Thumb	Pulgar	P
Index	Indice	I
Middle	Medio	M
Ring	Anular	A

2. With pick and fingers technique we use **pi** for the pick, **m** for the middle finger, **a** for the ring finger and **mi** for the pinky which comes from the Spanish name minique.

EXAMPLE 27:

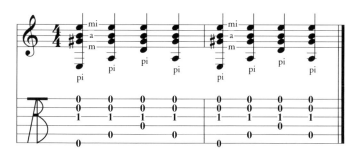

Practice bass line and chords separately to achieve a well balanced sound.

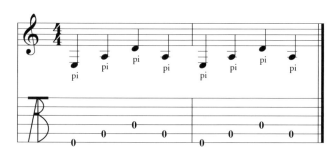
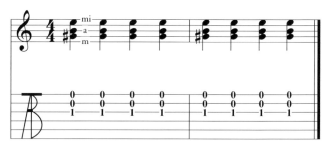

EXAMPLE 28: PLAYING IN 10TH's

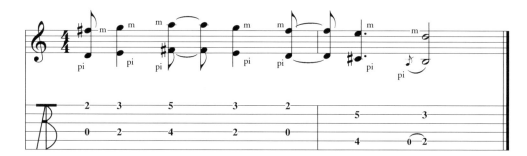

EXAMPLE 29:

EXAMPLE 31:

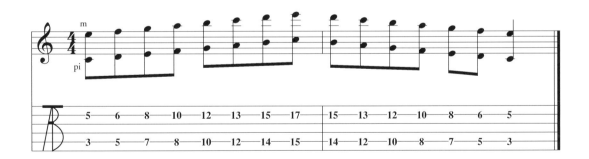

Chapter 6

"JOHN STOWELL—JAZZ MASTERY VOLUME II"

—*Transcribed by Chris Ullrich*—

The melodic minor scale equals a major scale with a ♭3.

EXAMPLE 1: D MAJOR SCALE

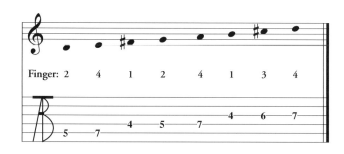

EXAMPLE 2: D MELODIC MINOR SCALE

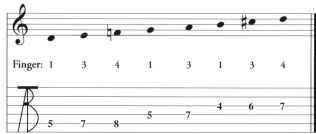

EXAMPLE 3: D MELODIC MINOR ACROSS ALL SIX STRINGS

EXAMPLE 4a: D MAJOR SCALE STARTING ON F♯ ON THE LOW E STRING

EXAMPLE 4b: D MELODIC MINOR SCALE STARTING ON F ON THE LOW E STRING

EXAMPLE 5: D MAJOR ARPEGGIO   D MELODIC MINOR ARPEGGIO

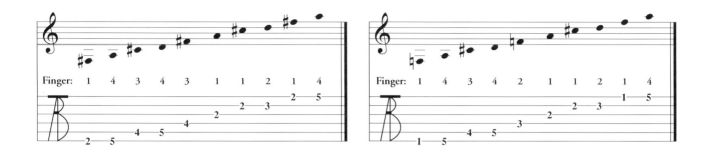

EXAMPLE 6: MINOR CHORDS

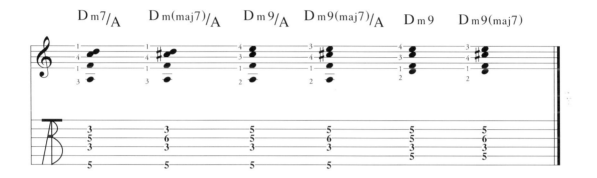

Dm7/A   Dm(maj7)/A   Dm9/A   Dm9(maj7)/A   Dm9   Dm9(maj7)

EXAMPLE 7: COMBINATION OF DORIAN + MELODIC MINOR

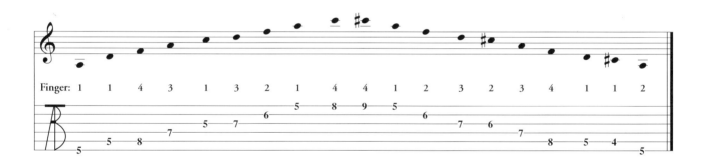

EXAMPLE 8: COMBINATION OF DORIAN + MELODIC MINOR

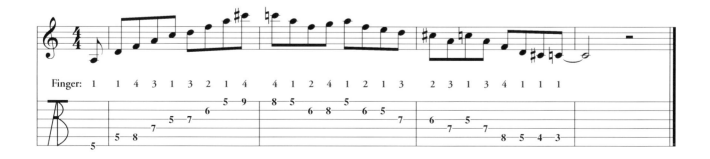

15

   Dominant = major scale with a ♭7 or a major chord with a ♭7

EXAMPLE 9: C DOMINANT SCALE/C MIXOLYDIAN

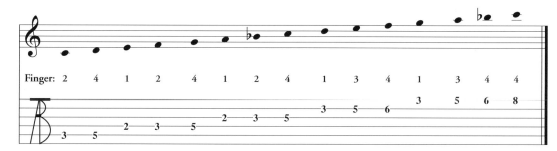

EXAMPLE 10: C DOMINANT ARPEGGIO OR C MIXOLYDIAN ARPEGGIO

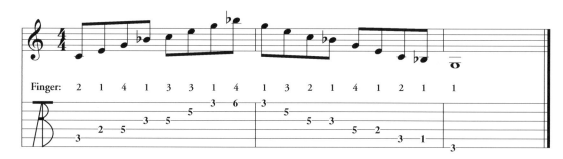

EXAMPLE 11: NAMING CHORDS

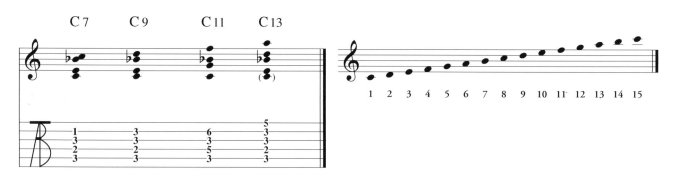

Dominant = 1 3 5 ♭7   **Extensions** = 9 11 13   **Alterations** = ♯5 ♭5/♯11 ♭9 ♯9

EXAMPLE 12:

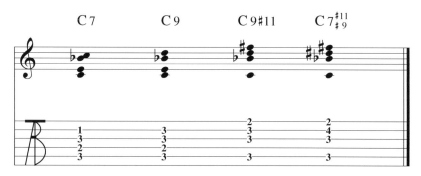

EXAMPLE 13:

EXAMPLE 14:

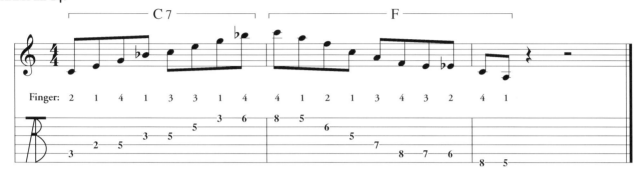

EXAMPLE 15:

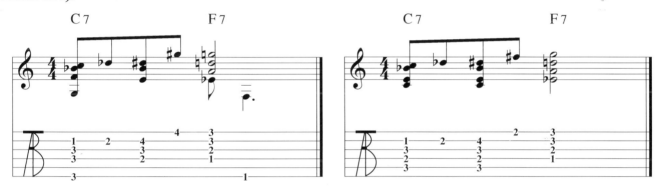

EXAMPLE 16:

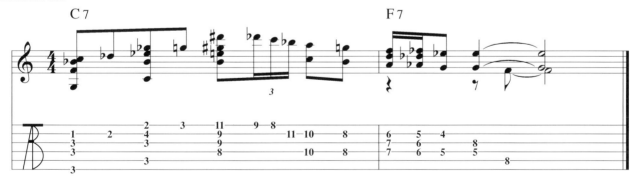

EXAMPLE 17:

EXAMPLE 18:

EXAMPLE 19:

EXAMPLE 20:

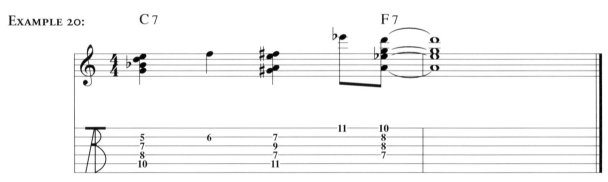

 Chapter 8

EXAMPLE 21: C7—USE THE MELODIC MINOR SCALE IN FOUR DIFFERENT KEYS

1. 1/2 Step ⇧ = C♯ melodic minor

2. 1 Step ⇩ = B♭ melodic minor

3. Perfect 4th ⇧ = F melodic minor

4. Perfect 5th ⇧ = G melodic minor

EXAMPLE 22: C♯ MELODIC MINOR (ALTERED DOMINANT, WHOLETONE DIMINISHED OR SUPER LOCRIAN SCALE)

C7 + C♯ MELODIC MINOR

EXAMPLE 24a:

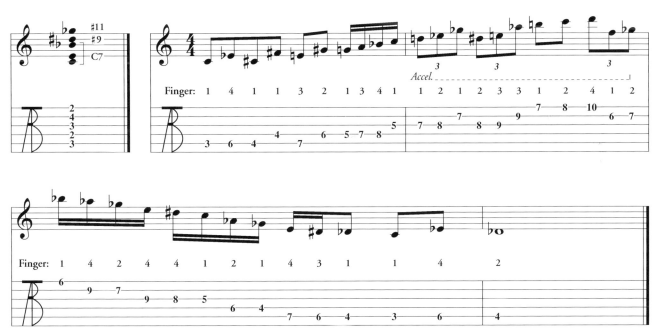

EXAMPLE 24b: COMBINATION OF C7 (C E G B♭) + C♯ MELODIC MINOR (C♯ E A♭ C)

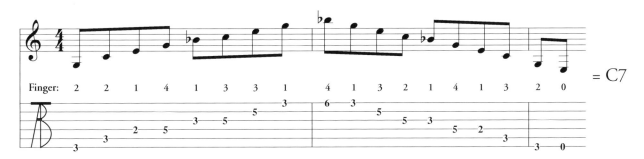

= C7

EXAMPLE 26:

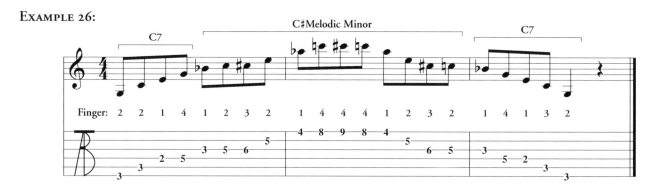

EXAMPLE 27:

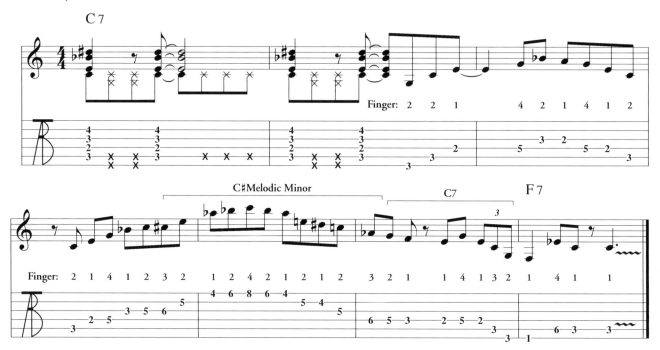

EXAMPLE 28: C♯ MELODIC MINOR WITH C7 RESOLVING TO F7

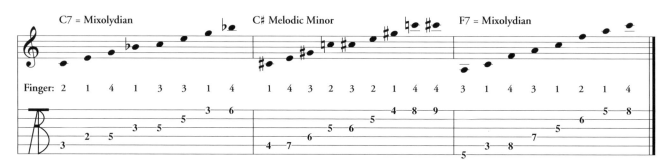

Example 29:

Example 30:

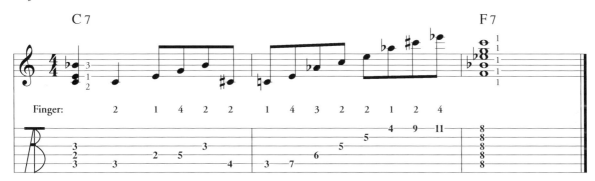

 Chapter 9

ONE WHOLE TONE BELOW C7

Example 31: B♭ Melodic Minor

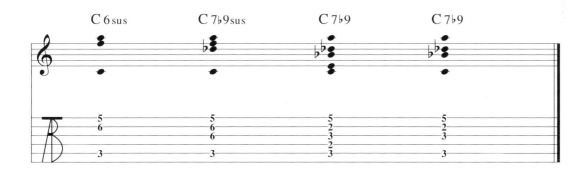

Example 32:

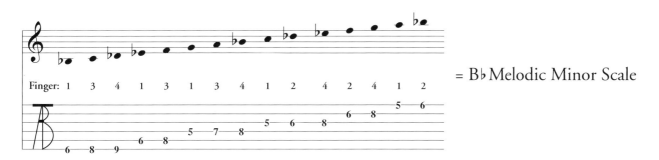

= B♭ Melodic Minor Scale

Example 33: Bb Melodic Minor Arpeggio

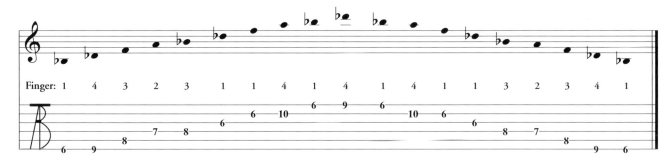

Example 34: C7 Arpeggio

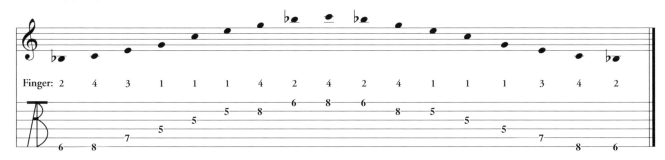

Example 35: Combining Bb Melodic Minor and C7

Example 36a:

Example 36b:

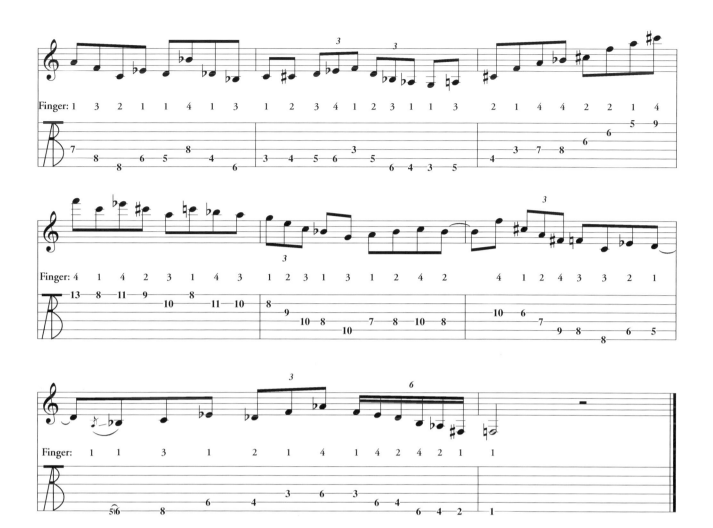

Example 37: B♭ Major Arpeggio

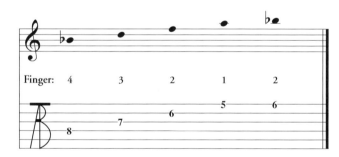

B♭ Melodic Minor Arpeggio

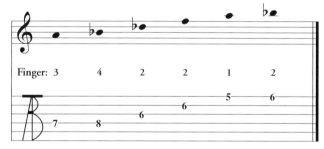

Example 38:

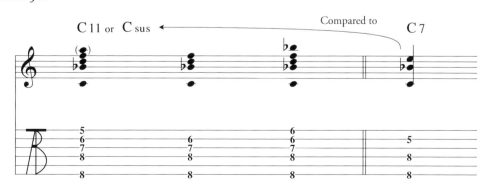

C 11 or C sus ← Compared to → C 7

These chords are created using a B♭ major arpeggio over a C7 chord.

Example 39: B♭ Major Arpeggio

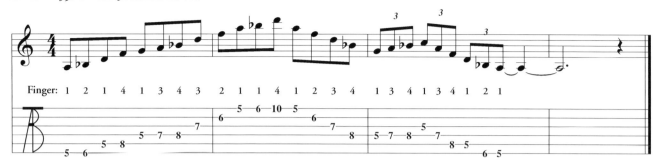

Example 40a:

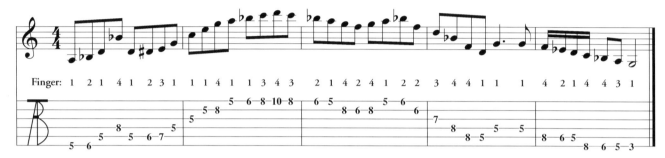

Example 40b:

Example 41: B♭ Major + B♭ Melodic Minor

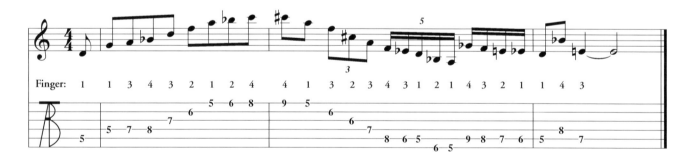

Example 42: B♭ Major + B♭ Melodic Minor

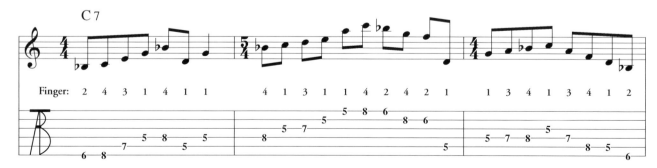

24

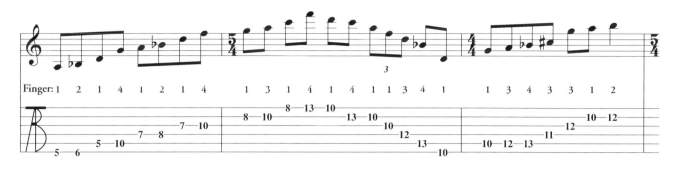

EXAMPLE 43: C11 (Bb MAJOR) + Bb MELODIC MINOR CHORDS

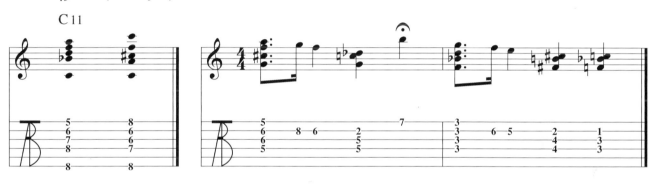

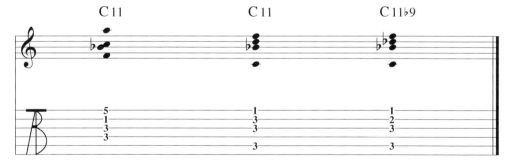

 **C7—F MELODIC MINOR A 4TH ABOVE >b6 ADDED**

EXAMPLE 44:

EXAMPLE 45: CHORDS

EXAMPLE 46: CHORDS

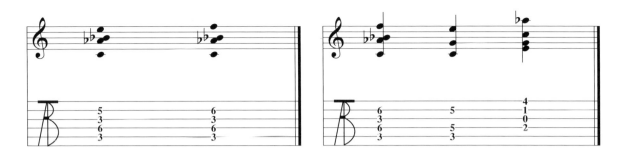

EXAMPLE 47a: C7 + F MELODIC MINOR

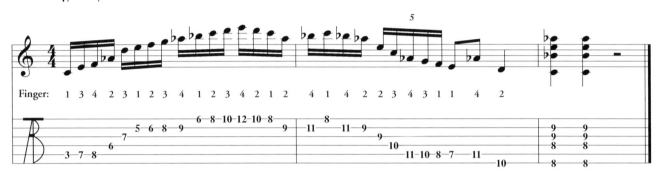

EXAMPLE 47b:

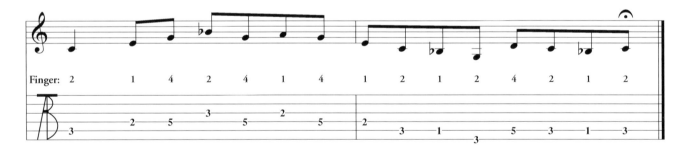

EXAMPLE 48: F MELODIC MINOR

Chapter 11

C7—G Melodic Minor a 5th Above > 9 ♯11 added

Example 49:

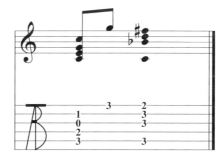

Example 50a: G Melodic Minor as Dominant C7

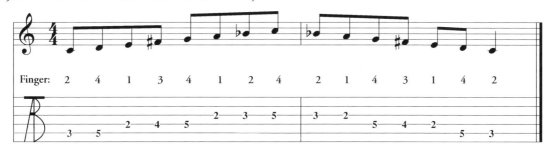

Example 50b:

Example 51:

C♯m9(maj7) → C♯m7 → C♯m9 → C♯m9(maj7)   C♯m9(maj7) as C7

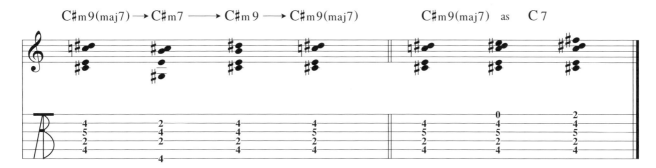

Example 52a: Chords in four keys—C♯, B♭, F and G

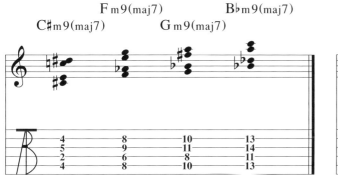

Example 52b: With Open E String on Top

EXAMPLE 53a:

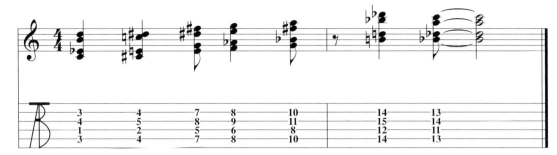

EXAMPLE 53b:

EXAMPLE 54:

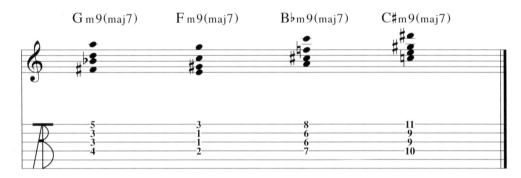

EXAMPLE 55a: COMBINING TWO CHORDS IN 4ᵀᴴˢ AS C7

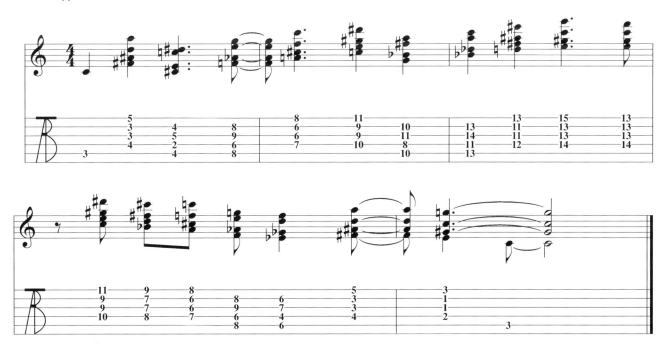

Chapter 12

EXAMPLE 1: TAPE 2 REVIEW

C7:   C♯—Play a melodic minor scale a 1/2 step **above** which gives you a C7 with a ♭9, ♯9, ♯11/♭5 and ♯5/♭13

       B♭—Play a melodic minor scale a whole step **below** which gives you a C7 with a ♭9, ♯9, 11 and 13

       F—Play a melodic minor scale a 4th **above** which gives you a C7 with a 9, 11, ♯5/♭13

       G—Play a melodic minor scale a 5th **above** which gives you a C7 with a 9, ♯11 and 13

Chapter 13

EXAMPLE 2: C HARMONIC MINOR SCALE

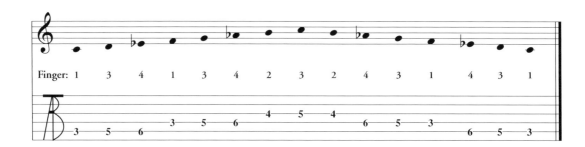

EXAMPLE 2: C HARMONIC MINOR SCALE—TWO OCTAVES

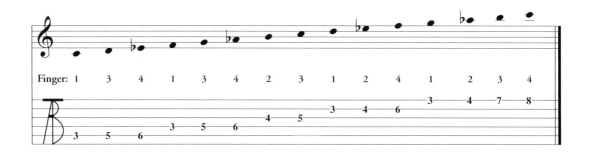

Play C harmonic minor over a C minor chord, but as a substitute chord/scale use over a dominant chord.

C7:   C♯ harmonic minor—Play a harmonic minor scale a 1/2 step **above** which gives you a C7 with a♭9, ♯9, ♯11/♭5, ♯5 and 13

EXAMPLE 4a: C♯ HARMONIC MINOR

EXAMPLE 4b: C7 OR C MIXOLYDIAN

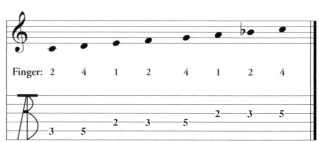

Example 5: C♯ Harmonic Minor + C Mixolydian

Example 6:

B♭ harmonic minor generates the same tensions as B♭ melodic minor (♭9, ♯9), and gives you the ♯11 (actually the ♭5th).

Example 7: B♭ Harmonic Minor

Example 8:

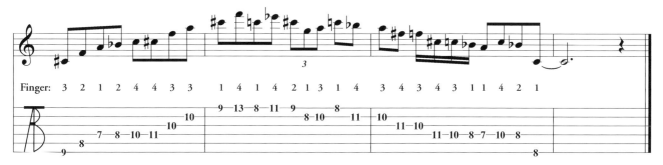

F harmonic minor generates the ♯5/♭13 and the ♭9 over a C7 chord.

EXAMPLE 9: F HARMONIC MINOR

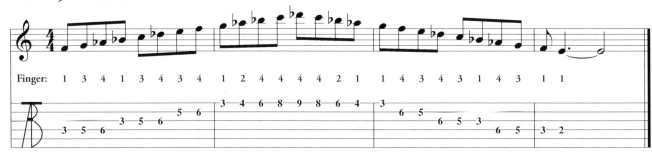

EXAMPLE 10: F HARMONIC MINOR + C7 COMBINED

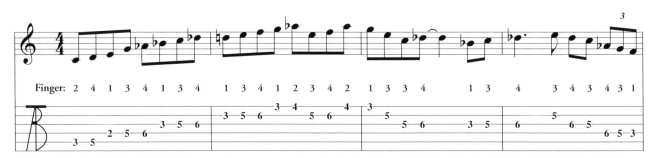

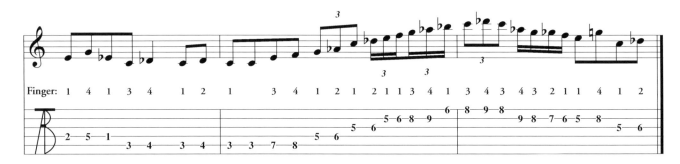

EXAMPLE 11a: G HARMONIC MINOR

EXAMPLE 11b: G HARMONIC MINOR + C7 COMBINED

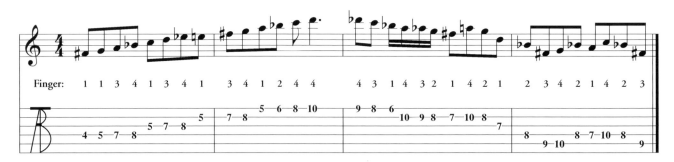

32

EXAMPLE 12: C♯ HARMONIC MINOR CHORDS

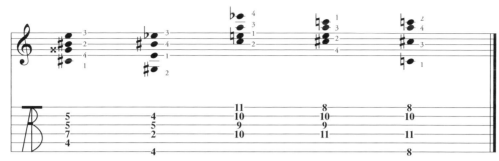

 Chapter 14

USING MAJOR TRIADS TO EXTEND DOMINANT 7TH CHORD

Nine triads work over a dominant 7th chord.

Interesting dichotomy—simple sound (pure) that sounds dissonant.

EXAMPLE 13:

1. C major	1	3	5
2. C♯ major	♭9	11	♯5/♭13
3. D major	9	♯11/♭5	6/13
4. E♭ major	♯9	5	♭7
5. F major	11	6/13	1
6. F♯ major	♯11/♭5	♭7	♭9
7. A♭ major	♯5/♭13	1	♯9
8. A major	6/13	♭9	3
9. B♭ major	♭7	9	11

EXAMPLE 14:

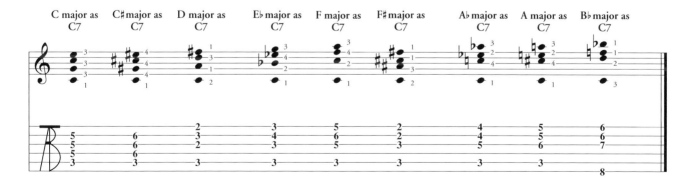

If the above chords work, lines derived from these chords will also work.

Example 15: B♭ Major Combined with C7

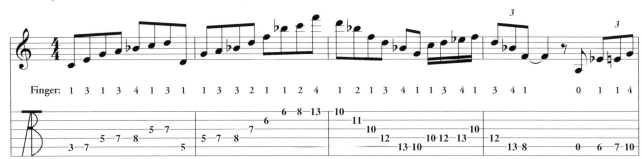

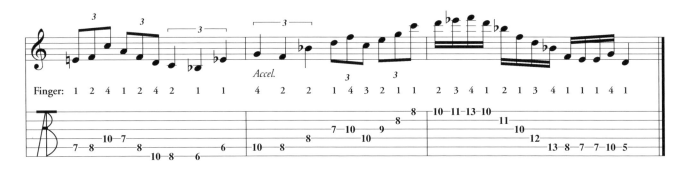

Example 16: A Major Combined with C7 (13, ♭9)

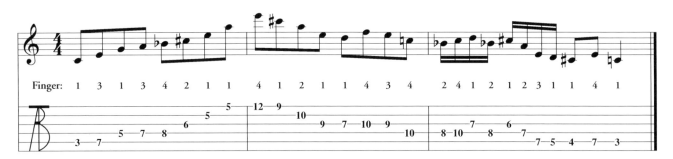

Example 17: A Major + B♭ Major Combined with C7

Example 18: C♯ Major + B♭ Major Combined with C7

EXAMPLE 19:

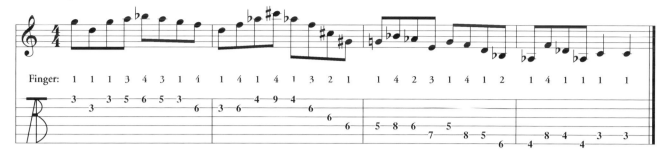

Finger: 1 1 1 3 4 3 1 4   1 4 1 4 1 4 3 2 1   1 4 2 3 1 4 1 2   1 4 1 1 1 1

EXAMPLE 20: A Major Triad + B♭ Melodic Minor Combined with C7 (13, ♭9, ♯9)

Finger: 1 3 1 3 4 2 2 1   3 4 1 1 2 3 2 1   1 4 1 4 1 3 4 2

Finger: 1 1 2 4 1 2 1 1   3 1 4 1 2 3 2 1   1 4 1

 Chapter 15

DOMINANT 7ᵀᴴ CHORDS

EXAMPLE 21a:

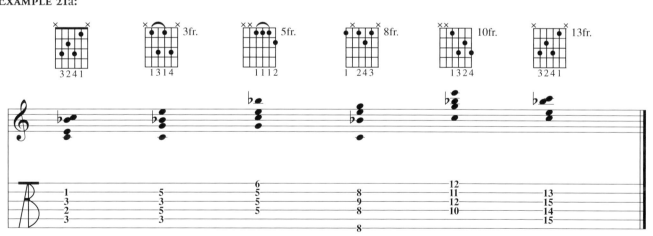

	(A)	(B)
7ᵗʰ Chord = 1 3 5 ♭7	**EXTENSIONS**	**ALTERATIONS**
	9	♯5
	11	♭5
	13	♯9
		♭9

Expand on the voicings in example #21a to make 9th chords

EXAMPLE 21b:

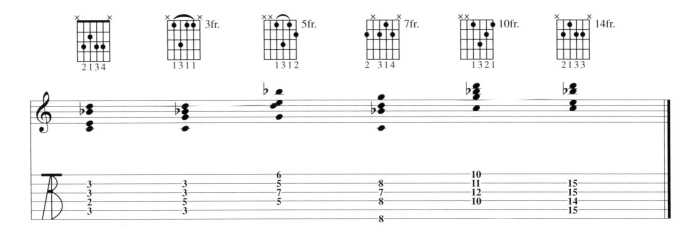

EXAMPLE 22: LOCATING ALTERATIONS

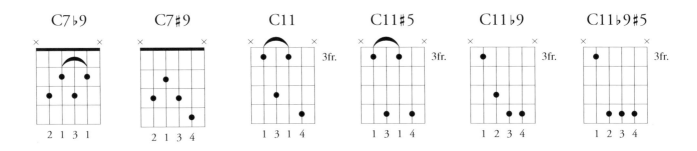

C7♭9   C7♯9   C11   C11♯5   C11♭9   C11♭9♯5

All of the chords below work as substitutions for C7 (Examples 23 and 24).

EXAMPLE 23:

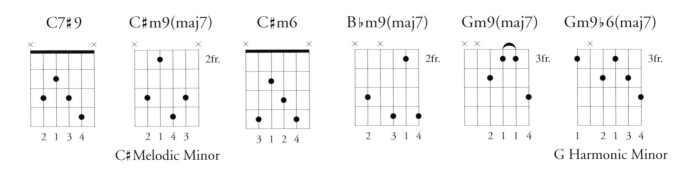

C7♯9   C♯m9(maj7)   C♯m6   B♭m9(maj7)   Gm9(maj7)   Gm9♭6(maj7)

C♯ Melodic Minor   G Harmonic Minor

EXAMPLE 24:

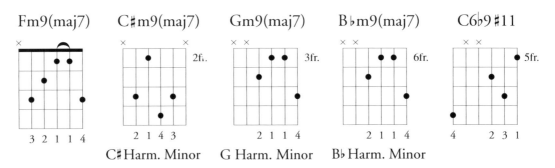

Fm9(maj7)   C♯m9(maj7)   Gm9(maj7)   B♭m9(maj7)   C6♭9♯11

C♯ Harm. Minor   G Harm. Minor   B♭ Harm. Minor

MAJOR 7TH CHORDS

Raise the B♭ of a C7th chord to B♮ to create a major 7th chord.

EXAMPLE 25:

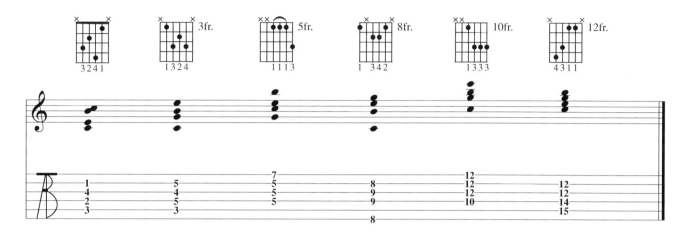

Major 7th Chord = 1 3 5 7

EXTENSIONS
6/13
9

ALTERATIONS
♯5
♭5/♯11

EXAMPLE 26: EXTENSIONS AND ALTERATIONS OF MAJOR 7TH VOICINGS

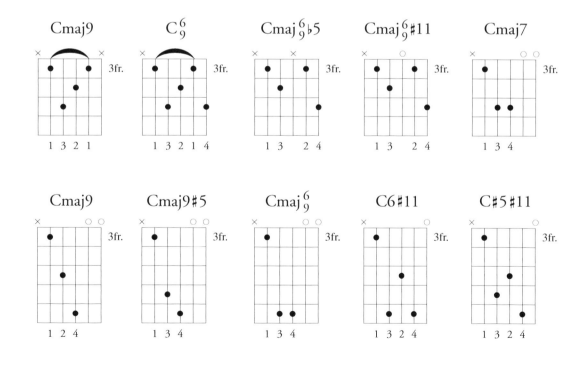

JOHN STOWELL

John Stowell began his successful career in the early 1970's with guitar lessons in his native Connecticut from guitarist Linc Chamberland, and from pianist John Mehegan, a respected jazz educator at the Juilliard School of Music and Yale University. Several years later he met noted bassist David Friesen in New York City, and they formed a duo that recorded and toured prolifically for seven years, with performances in Europe, Canada, the United States and Australia. The duo continues to perform thirty years after their first meeting .

In 1983 John and David Friesen joined flutist Paul Horn and Paul's son Robin Horn for a historic tour of the Soviet Union. This was the first time in forty years that an American jazz group had been invited to play public performances in Russia. In 1993, 1995 and 1998 John returned to Russia, playing in numerous cities. His two sold-out performances in Kursk may be the first appearances there by an American jazz musician.

John continues to tour, record and teach internationally. He has been Artist-In Residence at Schools in Germany, Indonesia, Argentina and in the United States and Canada. He served as assistant director and performer in Oregon Public Broadcasting's PDX Jazz Summit in 1991, and since 1995 has been a contributing columnist to a number of magazines, including *Downbeat, Guitar Player, Canadian Musician, Soundcheck* (Germany), and *Guitar Club* (Italy).

EXCELLENCE IN MUSIC

MEL BAY®

Since 1947

Made in the USA
Middletown, DE
26 April 2021